This book belongs to:

Name: _____
Email: _____
Phone: _____

Positive Habits Checklist

When you were born, your arms waved around wildly. You could not get them to go where you wished. Actually, in truth, you didn't even understand what your arms were. But it didn't take too long to solve the issue of how to command your hands and arms. You still benefit from that past learning experience now.

Habits are learned practices. Once you and your brain work out how to get something accomplished, your brain saves the practice, so you can do it again and again. Driving an auto-pilot, eating a meal, and reading are all learned practices. It took an effort to learn these skills, but now you are able to play back these known patterns rather than starting from scratch every time.

If you think about it, habits are your brain's approach to time management. It may be exceedingly inefficient for you to consciously choose how to spend each and every minute of your day. Your conscious brain has better matters to attend to than solve the same issues again and again. So, it assigns habits to your subconscious to remember and apply the practices/habits.

As you are aware, unfortunately, your innate habit-forming abilities have a few significant setbacks. Occasionally your subconscious will learn inefficient, inexact, or ineffective practices and habits. You might determine, for example, that smoking is a good way to manage stress or that sounding off is the best way to earn attention. Of course, smoking and sounding off are not positive habits. To line up with reality and live a positive life, you have to eventually break and replace habits that have grave adverse side effects.

I've found, that thinking about habits in this way, makes the idea of trying to break an old habit or create a new one much more achievable. So, let's look at a range of other simple things you can try when it comes to filling your life with positive habits.

Getting Ready to Make Positive Changes

- ☐ Engage the help of other people to dramatically step-up your chances of success.

- ☐ Search for role models who've already accomplished what you want.

- ☐ Ask for advice or mentoring from others.

- ☐ Read great books on what it is you're looking to do and use what you learn from them.

- ☐ Think about joining a group of like-minded individuals who share compatible goals.

- ☐ Don't attempt to tackle a long-standing habit head-on by powering through it.

- ☐ Establish exactly why you want to make or break this specific habit. How will you feel if you do? What will change if you do?

- ☐ Decide which tools will help you make or break your habits best. A journal, a tracker, post-it notes, phone reminders, a money jar etc.

- ☐ Set an achievable goal that does not overwhelm you

- ☐ Decide how you will reward yourself along the way. Rewarding yourself will help to remind you how well you're doing.

- ☐ Do not wait for habits to form or break. Take daily action towards the desired result.

Breaking Bad Habits

- ☐ Accept and appreciate that you have choices. Learn to take responsibility for every action you take and every reaction you have.

- ☐ Never expect to break a bad habit in 24 hours. Be wary of anyone promising that this is possible.

- ☐ Be sure you're ready for change. Never decide to try and break a long-lasting bad habit on a whim. i.e. as a New Years' Resolution.

- ☐ Appreciate that you may take step backwards on your journey but that's okay and is not something to feel guilty or down about. All successful people fail.

- ☐ Set yourself a specific goal. The more specific about what you want, and why, the better.

- ☐ Find or create positive reminders that will help you to remember why you're doing what you're doing.

- ☐ Set a date for starting the change. Put your commitment in writing so it is clear and is real to you.

- ☐ Use visualization. Visualize what your life will be like when you break your bad habit.

- ☐ Practice active diversion. Find something positive to replace your bad habit with. E.g. exercise or learning.

- ☐ Don't beat yourself up if you're not perfect all the time. It's not about perfection—it's about making progress one step at a time.

- ☐ Make contracts that reward you for fulfilling your efforts for breaking the habit. Write down the terms. I.e. "I will make a donation to charity in the amount of $___ for every packet of cigarettes I would have bought."

Making Positive Habits

- Choose habits that really interest and inspire you or will make a real difference to your life (or at least help to).
- Bring the habit you want to create into reality by writing it down.
- Don't put off until tomorrow what you can do today. If you believe something will make a positive difference to your life, why wait?
- Don't try and change everything in one go. Aim to take small action every day
- Remember: imperfect action is better than no action at all.
- Make a conscious decision to enjoy every step forward.
- Tell people what you're aiming for and, if possible, find an accountability partner.
- Know exactly what the habit is you're looking to create and try and establish how you'll know when you "get there".
- Make sure you have genuine, personal reasons for creating this habit. If it doesn't mean anything to you or it won't bring you joy, it will be a very hard journey.
- Understand that you're going to run into obstacles.
- Use positive reinforcements to keep you motivated, and to keep you going when we feel like quitting.
- There are many varieties of positive reinforcement - experiment and see which ones are really right for you.
- Keep track of how you're doing in a way that works for you.
- Adjust your goals according to how you're doing. If you're struggling, make the habit easier to create. If you find you no longer want to create the habit, change it.

Making Positive Habits

- Make a point of becoming a person of action in all areas of your life.
- When you've got a task to do, just do it.
- Celebrate each and every step you take and reward yourself often.
- Remember: if you've done it once, you can do it again.

Positive Habits for Getting Things Done

- Adjust targets for daily in advance. Choose what you'll accomplish; then accomplish it.
- To stop putting things off, learn to take on your most undesirable task first thing in the morning rather than delaying it till later.
- Establish your peak cycles of productiveness and schedule your most crucial jobs for those times.
- Set uninterruptible blocks of time for solo work where you have to concentrate.
- When you start a task, distinguish the target you have to reach before you can stop.
- Provide yourself a fixed period of time to make a dent in a job. Don't fret about how far you get. Simply put in the time.
- Batch like jobs like calls or errands together and knock them out in one session.

- Get up early in the morning and go straight to work on your most crucial job. You'll be able to often get more done prior to 8 A.M. than most individuals do in a total day.

- Intentionally pick up the pace and attempt to move a bit faster than usual. Walk quicker. Read quicker. Type quicker.

- Cut down stress by cultivating a relaxing, clutter-free house and office.

- Break procrastination by taking action right away after arranging a goal, even if the action isn't exactly planned out. You are able to always adjust your journey along the way.

- Arrange a deadline for task completion and use it as a focal point to remain track.

- Tell other people of your plans so that they'll hold you accountable.

- Always arrive ahead of time for appointments.

- Envision your goal as already achieved. Put yourself into a state of really being there.

- Provide yourself frequent rewards for accomplishment.

- At the finish of your workday, identify the first job you'll address tomorrow and set out the materials beforehand. The following morning start working on that job right away.

- Break complex jobs into smaller, well-defined jobs. Then focus on finishing just one of those jobs.

- Once you start a job, stick with it till it is 100% done. Don't shift tasks in the middle. When distractions arise, write them down to be handled later

12 Month Habit Tracker and Chocolate Coloring Pages

because

"Anything in Life is Better With Chocolate!"

-Kim Steadman

Month: _____

Day 1								
Day 2								
Day 3								
Day 4								
Day 5								
Day 6								
Day 7								
Day 8								
Day 9								
Day 10								
Day 11								
Day 12								
Day 13								
Day 14								
Day 15								
Day 16								
Day 17								
Day 18								
Day 19								
Day 20								
Day 21								
Day 22								
Day 23								
Day 24								
Day 25								
Day 26								
Day 27								
Day 28								
Day 29								
Day 30								

Month: _____

Day 1									
Day 2									
Day 3									
Day 4									
Day 5									
Day 6									
Day 7									
Day 8									
Day 9									
Day 10									
Day 11									
Day 12									
Day 13									
Day 14									
Day 15									
Day 16									
Day 17									
Day 18									
Day 19									
Day 20									
Day 21									
Day 22									
Day 23									
Day 24									
Day 25									
Day 26									
Day 27									
Day 28									
Day 29									
Day 30									

Month: _____

Day 1								
Day 2								
Day 3								
Day 4								
Day 5								
Day 6								
Day 7								
Day 8								
Day 9								
Day 10								
Day 11								
Day 12								
Day 13								
Day 14								
Day 15								
Day 16								
Day 17								
Day 18								
Day 19								
Day 20								
Day 21								
Day 22								
Day 23								
Day 24								
Day 25								
Day 26								
Day 27								
Day 28								
Day 29								
Day 30								

Month: _____

Day 1								
Day 2								
Day 3								
Day 4								
Day 5								
Day 6								
Day 7								
Day 8								
Day 9								
Day 10								
Day 11								
Day 12								
Day 13								
Day 14								
Day 15								
Day 16								
Day 17								
Day 18								
Day 19								
Day 20								
Day 21								
Day 22								
Day 23								
Day 24								
Day 25								
Day 26								
Day 27								
Day 28								
Day 29								
Day 30								

Month: _____

Day 1								
Day 2								
Day 3								
Day 4								
Day 5								
Day 6								
Day 7								
Day 8								
Day 9								
Day 10								
Day 11								
Day 12								
Day 13								
Day 14								
Day 15								
Day 16								
Day 17								
Day 18								
Day 19								
Day 20								
Day 21								
Day 22								
Day 23								
Day 24								
Day 25								
Day 26								
Day 27								
Day 28								
Day 29								
Day 30								

Month: _____

Day 1									
Day 2									
Day 3									
Day 4									
Day 5									
Day 6									
Day 7									
Day 8									
Day 9									
Day 10									
Day 11									
Day 12									
Day 13									
Day 14									
Day 15									
Day 16									
Day 17									
Day 18									
Day 19									
Day 20									
Day 21									
Day 22									
Day 23									
Day 24									
Day 25									
Day 26									
Day 27									
Day 28									
Day 29									
Day 30									

Month: _____

Day 1								
Day 2								
Day 3								
Day 4								
Day 5								
Day 6								
Day 7								
Day 8								
Day 9								
Day 10								
Day 11								
Day 12								
Day 13								
Day 14								
Day 15								
Day 16								
Day 17								
Day 18								
Day 19								
Day 20								
Day 21								
Day 22								
Day 23								
Day 24								
Day 25								
Day 26								
Day 27								
Day 28								
Day 29								
Day 30								

Month: _____

Day 1								
Day 2								
Day 3								
Day 4								
Day 5								
Day 6								
Day 7								
Day 8								
Day 9								
Day 10								
Day 11								
Day 12								
Day 13								
Day 14								
Day 15								
Day 16								
Day 17								
Day 18								
Day 19								
Day 20								
Day 21								
Day 22								
Day 23								
Day 24								
Day 25								
Day 26								
Day 27								
Day 28								
Day 29								
Day 30								

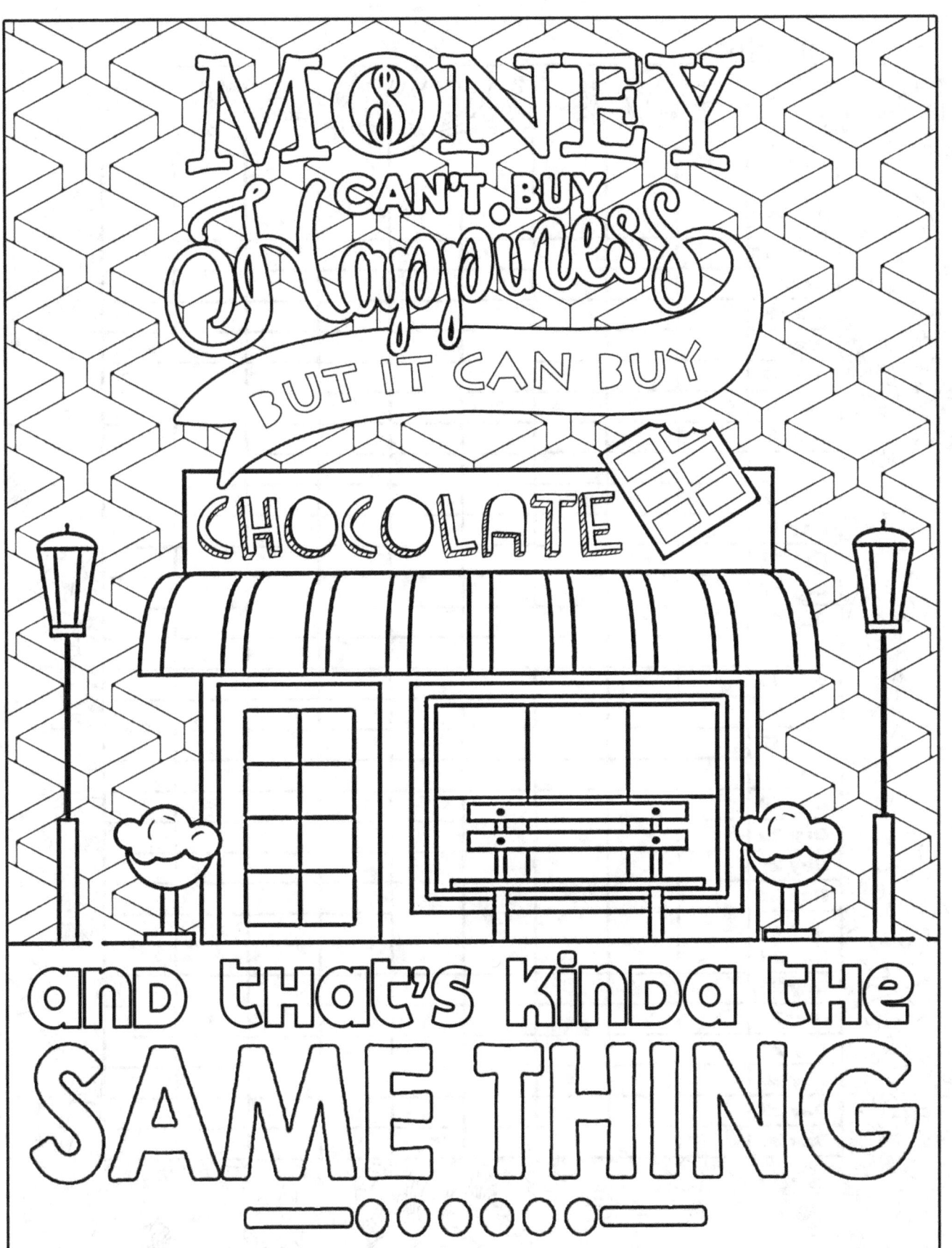

Month: _____

Day 1									
Day 2									
Day 3									
Day 4									
Day 5									
Day 6									
Day 7									
Day 8									
Day 9									
Day 10									
Day 11									
Day 12									
Day 13									
Day 14									
Day 15									
Day 16									
Day 17									
Day 18									
Day 19									
Day 20									
Day 21									
Day 22									
Day 23									
Day 24									
Day 25									
Day 26									
Day 27									
Day 28									
Day 29									
Day 30									

Month: _____

Day 1									
Day 2									
Day 3									
Day 4									
Day 5									
Day 6									
Day 7									
Day 8									
Day 9									
Day 10									
Day 11									
Day 12									
Day 13									
Day 14									
Day 15									
Day 16									
Day 17									
Day 18									
Day 19									
Day 20									
Day 21									
Day 22									
Day 23									
Day 24									
Day 25									
Day 26									
Day 27									
Day 28									
Day 29									
Day 30									

month: _____

Day 1									
Day 2									
Day 3									
Day 4									
Day 5									
Day 6									
Day 7									
Day 8									
Day 9									
Day 10									
Day 11									
Day 12									
Day 13									
Day 14									
Day 15									
Day 16									
Day 17									
Day 18									
Day 19									
Day 20									
Day 21									
Day 22									
Day 23									
Day 24									
Day 25									
Day 26									
Day 27									
Day 28									
Day 29									
Day 30									

Month: _____

Day 1									
Day 2									
Day 3									
Day 4									
Day 5									
Day 6									
Day 7									
Day 8									
Day 9									
Day 10									
Day 11									
Day 12									
Day 13									
Day 14									
Day 15									
Day 16									
Day 17									
Day 18									
Day 19									
Day 20									
Day 21									
Day 22									
Day 23									
Day 24									
Day 25									
Day 26									
Day 27									
Day 28									
Day 29									
Day 30									

Month: _____

Day 1								
Day 2								
Day 3								
Day 4								
Day 5								
Day 6								
Day 7								
Day 8								
Day 9								
Day 10								
Day 11								
Day 12								
Day 13								
Day 14								
Day 15								
Day 16								
Day 17								
Day 18								
Day 19								
Day 20								
Day 21								
Day 22								
Day 23								
Day 24								
Day 25								
Day 26								
Day 27								
Day 28								
Day 29								
Day 30								

About the Creator of This Book

When she's not sweeping dog hair, cooking, or doodling on paper, Kim C. Steadman writes and mentors authors. She is a freelance writer, teacher and ministers alongside her family in Grand Prairie, TX. Her books include prayer journals and children's books. Follow her prayerful writing world at KimSteadman.com

She loves coffee, chocolate, TexMex food and vacationing in the mountains. She also enjoys DIY projects that don't include power saws.

If you are a Jesus follower and write in any capacity, you are welcomed in the Write More; Write Now club. WriteMoreWriteNow.com is her hope to encourage everyone to push through self-doubt and write your words!

For more planners and journals visit KimSteadman.com

© 2019 Kim Steadman, dba Lifter Upper

ISBN: 9781687569202

www.ingramcontent.com/pod-product-compliance
Lightning Source LLC
Chambersburg PA
CBHW081707220526
45466CB00009B/2904